The Better Sweater
Knitting with Gwen Byrne

Book One:
Unique Patterns
for Novice through Expert

Arbor House   New York

Manufactured in the United States of America

10 9 8 7 6 5 4 3 2 1

Library of Congress Cataloging in Publication Data

Byrne, Gwen.
    The better sweater.

    1. Sweaters. 2. Knitting—Patterns. I. Title.
TT825.B96 1986   746.9′2   86-17348
ISBN 0-87795-845-9 (pbk.: v. 1)

Design by Laura Hough

Preface

I learned to knit when I was about three years old. It was a competitive necessity. I had two older sisters who made the most beautiful dolls' clothes, so I was intensely eager to share the joy and creativity of knitting.

I lived in Africa, where the vivid colors of the natural landscape and its inhabitants deluged my senses. Every new season brought its own color drama.

I spent many summer vacations on sheep farms with my mother's relatives. Here I absorbed the beginning of the wool story. We would often play in the huge warehouses filled with yarn bales, only to be reprimanded by our parents. They knew that puff adders also like wool bales!

Now, many years later, as I step into a yarn store I always enjoy that familiar smell. Perhaps that is one of the reasons I own a yarn store. Another reason is that I love the colors and textures in the glorious fibers that are available now. I encourage all my customers to play with the yarns, combining the various textures. So many happy people have returned, displaying their finished products, ready for another experimental project.

Part of the knitting experience is also the sense of accomplishment as you work on more and more difficult sweaters. This book is planned to assist you to move from the easy projects to the more complicated ones.

Many friends have given me endless support and encouragement during the birth and growth of this book: my sister Elizabeth, who knew of my talent before I recognized it; my editor, Susan Friedland, who knew what I could do with colors and yarns, but had to learn what I could do with written instructions; Susan Lombardo Kuhlman, who knew about cameras and light; Claire Timoney, Diane Davidson Porter, Fred Jackson, Jim Esposito, and Jay Kuhlman, who laughed even under the hot lights. What fun we had!

Many others read and reread the pattern instructions. Customers knitted the sweaters, so I know that all the designs are foolproof.

To these friends and all the many others involved, my thanks. Here it is at last!

Contents

BASICS AND TECHNIQUES

As your friends find out that you are learning to knit, you will discover from them that each step in knitting may have a variety of techniques. I teach what I believe to be the simplest method.

To start, you need one ball of medium-weight yarn (sport or worsted weight without knots or hairy slubs, please) and a pair of 10-inch #9 single-point knitting needles.

Casting On

1. Wrap the yarn twice around two fingers and pull the lower thread up through the center to form a slip knot. Place this loop onto a knitting needle, tightening it to slide easily on the needle. Hold this needle in your left hand.
2. Insert the right-hand needle through the loop from the front to the back.
3. Wrap the yarn from under, around the right needle. Holding the yarn tightly, bring the yarn through the slip knot until this loop is about 1½ inches long.
4. Slip this loop onto the left needle to form the second stitch.
5. Insert the right-hand needle in between the first and second stitches, tightening the first stitch, and repeat Step 3. All the stitches should be the same size as the needle.

Continue like this until you have cast on 20 stitches for your first sample.

Place the needle containing the stitches in your left hand.

The Knit Stitch (k st)

1. With the yarn hanging in the back, insert the right-hand needle into the first stitch from front to back. Wrap the yarn from under, around the right-hand needle.
2. Holding the yarn tightly, bring the yarn through the stitch, forming a new stitch on the right-hand needle, and slide the first stitch off the left-hand needle.
3. Repeat Steps 1 and 2 until all the stitches are on the right-hand needle.
4. Place the needle with the stitches in your left hand and continue with Steps 1 and 2.

When this stitch is used in every row, it is called garter stitch and is distinguishable by the ridges it forms on both sides of your sample.

The Purl Stitch (p st)

1. With the yarn hanging in the front, insert the right-hand needle into the first stitch from the back toward the front. Wrap the yarn over and around the right-hand needle.
2. Holding the yarn tightly, bring the needle through the stitch toward the back, forming a

new stitch on the right-hand needle, and slide the first stitch off the left-hand needle.
3. Repeat Steps 1 and 2 until all the stitches are on the right-hand needle.
4. Place the needle with the stitches in your left hand and continue with Steps 1 and 2.

The purl stitch is used in combination with the knit stitch; it is rarely used on its own. The stitch formed when working one row of knit and one row of purl alternately is called stockinette stitch (st st).

Work about 3 inches of stockinette stitch on your sampler and try to recognize which side is the knit side and which the purl.

Knit side: rows of V's.

Purl side: rows of loops.

By this time you probably realize that part of the art of knitting is holding the yarn with even tension so that all the stitches are the same size.

My method puts the little finger of the right hand to work, and sometimes it objects painfully. Practice, and an even group of stitches will soon replace the pain with pride.

Holding the Yarn

1. Four inches from your stitches, scoop the yarn with your little finger from back to front.

2. Twist the hand so that the thread runs in the palm of your hand.
3. Bring the index finger under the thread, bend the other fingers, and you are ready. The index finger, with the yarn across the first joint, guides the yarn, and the little finger guides the tension of the knitting.

Use the little finger:

1. Bent, when you have enough yarn in your hand; and
2. Slightly raised, when you need to feed more yarn to the index finger.

All this will feel very clumsy at first, but the clumsiness will disappear after a while.

Combining knit and purl stitches on the same row to form ribs is called ribbing.

Ribbing

Ribbing, generally worked with a smaller needle, forms a natural border because of its elasticity. The sweater will hold its shape better at the hip, waist, wrist, and neck areas because of the ribbing.

Here are some examples:

1 × 1 Rib: *knit 1 stitch, purl 1 stitch*
k1, p1, —Repeat the stitches between the asterisks.

2 × 2 Rib: *knit 2 stitches, purl 2 stitches*
k2, p2 —Repeat the stitches between the asterisks.

This pattern will work correctly only if the yarn is at the correct place (either in front of the work or behind it) when needed.

An example of the 2 × 2 rib: k2, bring the yarn in between the two needles toward the front, and p2. Take the yarn in between the two needles toward the back, and k2. Repeat until all the stitches have been worked.

To shape the sweater, you will need to make sections larger or smaller; this means increasing or decreasing the number of stitches.

The Increase (inc)

On a knit row:

1. Insert the right-hand needle from front to back into the loop of the stitch below the next stitch to be knitted.
2. Place this extra loop on the left-hand needle and knit the 2 stitches separately (1 inc).

On a purl row:

1. Insert the right-hand needle from front to back into the loop of the stitch below the next stitch to be purled.

2. Place this extra loop on the left-hand needle, twisting the stitch toward the front, and purl the 2 stitches separately (1 inc).

This method of increasing is the easiest and the least obvious. Various other methods leave large and unsightly holes.

To make a section of a sweater smaller means reducing the number of stitches. This is called decreasing, and here you need to know more than one technique.

The Decrease (dec)— work 2 stitches (sts) together (tog)

On a knit row:

Insert the needle through 2 sts as to knit (knitwise). Knit them tog to form 1 st. This stitch slants to the right.

On a purl row:

Insert the needle through 2 sts as to purl (purlwise). Purl them tog to form 1 st.

The Decrease—slip (sl) a stitch

On a knit row:

1. Insert the needle into the st as to knit. Slip the st from the left-hand needle to the right (sl 1).
2. Knit the next stitch.
3. Insert the tip of the left-hand needle into the slip stitch (sl st) from left to right toward the front, holding the yarn tightly so that the knit stitch (k st) does not slide off the needle. Pass the sl st over the k st, and drop it off the needle. This stitch slants to the left.

On a purl row:

1. Insert the needle into the st as if to purl. Slip the st from the left-hand needle to the right (sl 1).
2. Purl the next st.
3. Insert the tip of the left-hand needle into the slip stitch (sl st) from left to right, toward the front, holding the yarn tightly so that the purl stitch (p st) does not slide off the needle. Pass the sl st over the p st, and drop it off the needle.

Adding New Yarn

At some point you will need to add new yarn when one skein is finished.

Always add yarn at the beginning (beg) of a row. This method can be used when attaching yarn of the same color or of another color for stripes.

1. Drop the old yarn.
2. Leaving about 8 inches of the new skein hanging, put the needle into the first stitch. Make a loop, place this onto the right-hand needle, and knit the first stitch. Finish the row.
3. Tie the new and the old threads together, tightening the few loose sts at the beg of the row. These dangling threads will be used in the finishing of the seams of your sweater. Never tie double knots, please!

To remove all the stitches from the needles with a finished edge (which prevents the sts from unraveling), you bind off.

Binding Off

Always try to bind off on the knit side, as follows:

1. Knit 2 sts.
2. Insert the left-hand needle into the front of the first st knitted, from left to right. Pass the stitch over the second stitch and drop it off the needle. This is 1 st bound off.
3. Knit 1 more stitch and repeat Step 2. Hold the thread tightly when passing one stitch over the other, but try to keep the stitches as loose as possible.

When one last stitch remains, cut the thread, leaving about 10 inches, and pull the thread through the stitch. This thread is used to sew the seams.

NOTE: When binding off, you always need 2 sts on the right-hand needle.

Binding Off in Pattern

On a k2, p2 rib, bind off as follows:
k2, bind off 1 st, bring the yarn to the front, p1, take the yarn to the back, bind off 1 st. Repeat, knitting the knit stitches and purling the purl stitches.

Asterisks

These are indicators advising that the instructions within the asterisks are to be repeated. For example:
k2, p1, k2 repeat 1 ×. This means k2, p1, k2, k2, p1, k2.

If no specific number of repeats is indicated, just repeat the instructions to the end of the row.

Yarn Over (yo)

Yarn over is used to make buttonholes or lacy eyelet stitches.

When the following stitch is a knit stitch:

From the back, wrap the yarn over and under the needle toward the back, leaving 1 slanted st across the needle.

When the following stitch is a purl stitch:

From the front, wrap the yarn over and under the needle toward the front.

Buttonholes

Here are two methods. Use the first for small buttons.

FIRST METHOD

Work a few sts from the edge, yarn over (yo), k2 tog, work to the end of the row. On the following row, remember to knit or purl the yarn over as your pattern indicates.

SECOND METHOD

Work to the correct position in the pattern (usually 2 to 4 sts from the edge), sl 1, k1, pass the sl st over (psso). Turn your needles so that the work is facing in the opposite direction and cast on 2 sts. Turn the needles back to the original position and k2 tog, pulling the thread quite tightly so that no holes are formed. Continue in pattern to the end of the row.

Work the next row in pattern as established before the buttonhole.

Stitch Gauge

Knitting a sample swatch to make a stitch gauge is probably the most important step when knitting a sweater. The stitch gauge is the measurement you require to tell you how many stitches equal 1 inch, and how many rows equal 1 inch. This information determines the number of stitches you will need to make your sweater the correct size.

All instructions in this book, and in other books or magazines, base the sizing of a sweater (or other garment) on the combination of the weight (thickness) of the yarn used, the size of the needles, and the determined stitch gauge. The smaller the needles and the thinner the yarn, the more stitches and rows it will take to make 1 inch. When the needles are bigger and the yarn is thicker, you will require fewer stitches and rows per inch.

The stitch gauge is usually given for 4 inches. A swatch of this size is more accurate than a smaller one.

Never measure the gauge by the border or rib stitch; this would not be an accurate measurement. Always use the larger needles and the

stitch suggested for the body of the sweater to make a swatch.

Making a Swatch

Using the needles, yarn, and stitch pattern specified in the instructions, cast on the number of sts for 4 inches plus 4 extra sts. Work a swatch about 4 inches long. Bind off all the sts. Smooth out the sample on a table. *DO NOT STRETCH THE SWATCH.*

Using a knit measure gauge (more accurate than a tape measure), measure the required number of stitches and the required number of rows. If your swatch is smaller than 4 inches wide, change to larger needles and knit a new swatch. Check the gauge again. If the swatch is larger than 4 inches wide, change to smaller needles and repeat the procedure. Measure the swatch again. Repeat this until the gauge is correct.

This procedure should never be omitted. Always knit a swatch. It is far more sensible to take the time to knit a swatch than to rip a too small or too large sweater later.

Picking Up Stitches

Stitches are picked up to create a border around the armholes or neck, or the fronts of a cardigan.

A circular needle 16 inches long is used for crew necks and one 24 inches long is used for V necks.

1. Starting at the left shoulder, with the right side of the sweater facing you, insert the needle 1 st from the edge, straight through toward the back. Wrap the yarn around the needle and bring this st through to the front. Repeat this step until all the sts have been picked up on the side edge.
2. At the center front of the neck and along the back, the bound-off sts are treated in the same way. The needle is inserted under both sides of the bound-off stiches.

This is a tricky procedure. One hint is to keep the needle tip short so that the distance between the sts on the needle and the st to be picked up is minimal.

3. When all the sts are on the needle, place a ring marker on the needle to show the beginning of the round. Start working in the pattern as instructed. These sts are always worked in rounds. Do not turn the needles back and forth after the round is completed.
4. For armhole borders, use straight single-pointed needles. Use circular needles only if the side seams of the sweater have been sewn together.

Markers

Markers are used to indicate special places on a garment, such as armholes. There are two kinds of markers:

1. A piece of thread or a coil marker, which are used for armhole indicators. These markers will be removed when the sweater is being sewn together.
2. For division on a knitting needle, as an indicator of a certain number of stitches or a stitch pattern, use a regular flat ring marker. This does not get knitted into the sweater but moves from needle to needle as you work. It is a cue to you that the pattern stitch changes.

Measuring

Always measure any piece of the sweater straight up or sideways, never at an angle. To measure the width while you are working, work the border and 3 inches of the sweater. Spread the work onto two needles and then measure the width. Now you can tell what the piece measures before it reaches the required length and you realize that it is too small or too large.

Lengths, not only widths, are important. If you are long-waisted or short-waisted, changes have to be made. This length adjustment is generally made before the armhole shaping or before the marker is placed in position.

To make measuring an armhole length easier, you can follow the colored thread hint. When you work the first decrease on the sleeve, work along with your yarn a 10-inch thread of another color, knitting about 10 sts in the middle of the row. This forms an obvious line, which makes measuring the armhole length or the sleeve cap very easy. This thread is removed when the sleeve has been set into the sweater.

Sewing a Sweater Together

When putting a sweater together, always work at a table—a flat surface is much better than a bed or a rug.

The first step is to pin the pieces together with sturdy straight pins. Begin with the shoulders: starting at the arm edge, with the right sides of the pieces facing each other, place one or two pins. Next, pin the neck edge. Finally, ease and pin the center pieces of fabric. Continue in this fashion with all the pieces: always pinning the outer edges first, and then easing and pinning the midsections.

To sew, use a blunt-tip embroidery needle or yarn needle and threads hanging from the sweater, if possible. Using a running stitch, insert the needle one stitch from the edge, from the front through both pieces of work, to the back. Pull the needle and thread through. Then insert the needle from the back to the front into the very next stitch, *never skip any stitches*, pull the needle and thread through to the front. Repeat until the seam is complete. Tension of the stitch should allow the same elasticity as exists in the garment. When you run out of thread, weave the needle and thread backward through the top of the seam and cut the end that remains. When attaching a new thread, repeat the last two inches sewn to create an overlap and prevent gaps in the seam.

When you want absolutely flat seams, to attach a pocket for example, use a back or over stitch.

Finishing a Drop-Shoulder Sweater

Most of the sweaters in this book are called drop-shoulder sweaters. These sweaters have no shaping or indentation for the armholes.

When putting a sweater together, always work at a table—a flat surface is much better than a bed or a rug.

The easiest method to finish this type of garment is as follows:

1. With the right sides of back and front facing, pin and sew the shoulder seams.
2. Open and lay out flat the back and front with the right side facing up. The yarn markers will still be attached to the sweater.

3. Fold the sleeve in half to find the center of the bound-off edge (the wider side of the length of the sleeve). With the right side facing down, pin the center of the bound-off edge of the sleeve to the shoulder seam of the sweater. The sleeve is now lying across the sweater, covering the neck opening. The bound-off edge of the sleeve will be parallel to the side edge of the sweater, lining up with the markers. Pin the sleeve into the area between the marker on the front and the marker on the back. Pin the body and the sleeve together, being careful not to stretch one side more than the other. Sew the seam.
4. Fold the sweater so that the right side is on the inside. Starting at the underarm, pin the sleeve seams and then the side seams. Sew the seams.

Yarn Substitution

Each sweater in this book has been made in the specified yarn. If this yarn is not available to you, ask your yarn store or supplier to recommend a substitute. In selecting a substitute, however, I have an added simple recommendation: buy one skein of a yarn you like, and go home and knit swatches with different needle sizes. This will serve two purposes: to make sure you can get the correct gauge and to feel the draping quality of the yarn. Following this procedure will eliminate all those ill-fitting garments that lie in the bottom of your drawers. If the gauge is correct but the swatch seems too sheer or too dense, choose another yarn. Refer to the Bellhop Jacket (page 000) to see what happens when two totally different yarns are used to make the same sweater. One version, made with a soft angora, drapes readily; the other, made of a heavier, dense cotton, does not drape at all. Both are beautiful, but the same pattern has yielded two quite different sweaters.

A Schematic

A schematic is a linear sketch of the garment and its shape. Along each edge is an arrow with an inch measurement. This tells you the width or length of any given section of the body or sleeve of the garment. Understanding the schematic serves two very important purposes:

1. It illustrates the shape of the piece you are knitting; it is especially useful if complicated shaping is required.
2. It helps you decide on the length or width or general size of any given part of the sweater in case you want to make adjustments.

PLEASE always read the schematic. It is a vital part of the sweater you are knitting. Understanding the schematic will erase the "my sweater does not fit" syndrome. Never knit happily along without checking the measurements.

Choosing a Size

Always refer to the FINISHED MEASUREMENTS before deciding on the size to knit. Large sweaters are fashionable now, and the size of the sweater does not correspond to your actual size. This should be considered when using all patterns from magazines and books.

Now that all the possible problems have been discussed, my wish is that your knitting hours are filled with exciting projects—and may all your sweaters be scene-stealers!

Abbreviations

beg	beginning
c n	cable needle
dec	decrease
decs	decreases
inc	increase
incs	increases
k	knit
p	purl
rev	reverse
r s	right side
sl	slip
sl 1, k1, psso	slip 1 stitch, knit 1 stitch, pass the slip stitch over
st	stitch
sts	stitches
st st	stockinette stitch
tog	together
wyib	with the yarn in the back
wyif	with the yarn in the front
w s	wrong side
yb	yarn back
yf	yarn forward
yo	yarn over
1 ×	one time

Patterns

BEGINNER

Cozy Rosy

SIZES: One size

FINISHED MEASUREMENTS: Bust 60 inches; total length 27 inches

MATERIALS:

(A) Charity Hill Bulky wool 5 (100 g/3.5 ounce) skeins, blue

(B) Berger du Nord Polaire 4 (50 g/1.75 ounce) skeins, used double-strand, lavender

Needles: #9, #10 single-point; #9 16-inch circular

GAUGE: 12 sts and 16 rows = 4 inches (3 sts = 1 inch; 4 rows = 1 inch)

STITCH PATTERN: Stockinette stitch

BACK

With smaller needles (#9) and A, cast on 90 sts. Work in k1, p1 rib for 2 inches. Change to larger needles (#10) and st st and work until the piece measures 15 inches. Place yarn or coil markers at each edge. Continue to work until the piece measures 27 inches in total. Bind off all sts loosely.

FRONT

Work the front the same as the back until the piece measures 4 inches. Change to B and in st st, using double strand, work for 7 inches. After the first B stripe, change back to A and work for 7 inches. (At 15 inches on the front, remember to place a yarn or coil marker.) Work another B stripe for 7 inches. Change back to A and work until the front measures the same as the back. Bind off all sts loosely.

SLEEVES

With smaller needles (#9) and A, cast on 40 sts. Work k1, p1 rib for 2 inches. Change to larger needles (#10) and st st. Increase 1 st at each edge on every knit row 18× until 76 sts. Continue to work across 76 sts until the sleeve measures 11 inches in total. Bind off all sts loosely.

FINISHING

1. With the right sides of back and front facing, pin and sew the shoulder seams.
2. Open and lay out flat the back and front with the right side facing up. The yarn markers will still be attached to the sweater.
3. Fold the sleeve in half to find the center of the bound-off edge (the wider side of the length of the sleeve). With the right side facing down, pin the center of the bound-off edge of the sleeve to the shoulder seam of the sweater.

The sleeve is now lying across the sweater, covering the neck opening. The bound-off edge of the sleeve will be parallel to the side edge of the sweater, lining up with the mark-ers. Pin the sleeve into the area between the marker on the front and the marker on the back. Pin the body and the sleeve together, being careful not to stretch one side more than the other. Sew the seam.

4. Fold the sweater so that the right side is on the inside. Starting at the underarm, pin the sleeve seams and then the side seams. Sew the seams.

5. Here are two variations for finishing the neck.

Turtleneck: With #9 16-inch circular needle and the right side facing you, start at the left shoulder seam and pick up 96 sts around the neck (48 sts in the front and 48 sts at the back). Work k1, p1 rib in rounds until the collar measures 8 inches or the desired length. Bind off loosely in ribbing.

Roll Neck: With # 9 16-inch circular needle and the right side facing you, pick up 90 sts around the neck. Work 10 rounds of knit stitch only. This will look like st st. Bind off loosely.

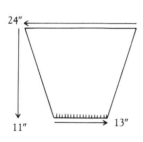

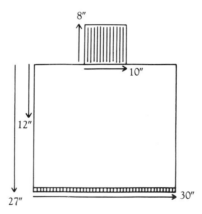

Regatta

SIZES: Medium, large; large size is in
  parentheses
FINISHED MEASUREMENTS: Chest
  44½ (48) inches; total length 25 (26) inches
MATERIALS:
  (A) Melrose Bongio 12 (14) (50 g/1.75
    ounce) skeins, navy
  (B) Melrose Bongio 2 (50g/1.75 ounce)
    skeins, gray
  Needles: #6, #8 single-point
GAUGE: 18 sts and 22 rows = 4 inches
    (4.5 sts = 1 inch; 5.5 rows = 1
    inch)
STITCH PATTERNS:
  #1: Stockinette stitch
  #2: k4, p4 rib as follows:
    Row 1: *k4, p4* repeat.
    Row 2: Knit the knits and purl the purls.
    Repeat these 2 rows.

BACK

With smaller needles (#6) and B, cast on 100
(106) sts. Work 2 rows k1, p1 rib. Change to A
and continue in k1, p1 rib until the piece measures 3 inches. Change to larger needles (#8)
and pattern stitch #1. Work until the piece
measures 13½ (14½) inches. Tie yarn markers at
each edge. Continue to work until the piece
measures 22 (23) inches. Change to pattern
stitch #2, alternating the colors as follows: 2
rows with B, 6 rows with A. Work until the total
back measures 25 (26) inches. Bind off all sts
loosely in pattern.

FRONT

Repeat the instructions for the back.

SLEEVES

With smaller needles (#6) and B, cast on 46 sts.
Work 2 rows k1, p1 rib. Change to A and continue in k1, p1 rib until the piece measures 3
inches. Change to larger needles (#8) and pattern stitch #1, and inc 14 sts evenly across the
first row. Working in pattern #2, inc 1 st at each
edge on every 5th row (work 4 rows and then the
inc row) 17 (20) ×. With 94 (100) sts work until
the sleeve measures 21 inches in total. Bind off
all sts loosely.

FINISHING

1. With the right sides of back and front facing,
   pin and sew the shoulder seams, leaving a 10-
   inch opening for the neck.
2. Open and lay out flat the back and front with
   the right side facing up. The yarn markers will

still be attached to the sweater.

3. Fold the sleeve in half to find the center of the bound-off edge (the wider side of the length of the sleeve). With the right side facing down, pin the center of the bound-off edge of the sleeve to the shoulder seam of the sweater. The sleeve is now lying across the sweater, covering the neck opening. The bound-off edge of the sleeve will be parallel to the side edge of the sweater, lining up with the markers. Pin the sleeve into the area between the marker on the front and the marker on the back. Pin the body and the sleeve together, being careful not to stretch one side more than the other. Sew the seam.

4. Fold the sweater so that the right side is on the inside. Starting at the underarm, pin the sleeve seams and then the side seams. Sew the seams.

5. Fold the boat neck toward the inside, rounding the edges, and sew down.

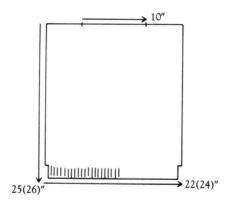

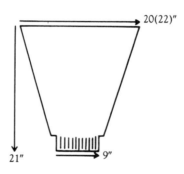

Sprinkles

SIZES: Small, medium; medium size is in parentheses

FINISHED MEASUREMENTS: Bust 40 (44) inches; total length 23 (25) inches

MATERIALS:
  Pingouin Jarré 12 (14) (50 g/1.75 ounce) skeins, black/white
  Needles: #7, #9 single-point; #7 16-inch circular
  2 stitch holders

GAUGE: 16 sts and 18 rows = 4 inches (4 sts = 1 inch; 4.5 rows = 1 inch)

STITCH PATTERN:
  Stockinette stitch

IMPORTANT HINT FOR SMOOTH RAGLAN EDGE DECREASES:
  Decrease 1 stitch in from the edge, never the first or the last stitch.

BACK

With smaller needles (#7), cast on 74 (80) sts. Work k1, p1 rib for 3 inches. Change to larger needles (#9) and st st, and inc 8 stitches evenly across the row (82 [88] sts). Work until the piece measures 13 (14) inches in total. On the first dec row, use about 12 inches of yarn in another color, knitting it along in the center of the row for about 10 stitches. This is used to assist in the measuring of the armhole. Shape the raglan armhole as follows: Dec 1 st at each edge on every knit row 25 (29) × until 32 sts remain and the armhole measures 10 (11) inches from the colored thread. Measure straight up, not at an angle. Place the remaining 32 sts on a st holder.

FRONT

Work the front the same as the back until the armhole measures 7 (8) inches. Shape the neck as follows: Place the center 20 sts on a st holder. Attach a new skein of yarn to the left shoulder (after the st holder) and, working the two sides of the front at the same time, dec at the NECK EDGE 1 st on every knit row 6×. Remember to continue the armhole shaping at the same time. When the armhole measures the same as the back armhole and 1 st remains, the front is complete.

SLEEVES

With smaller needles (#7), cast on 34 sts. Work k1, p1 rib for 3 inches. Change to larger needles (#9) and st st. Inc 14 sts evenly across the first knit row (48 sts). Working in st st, inc 1 st at each edge every 5th (4th) row (work 4 (3) rows and then the increase row) 12 (15) ×. Continue to work across 72 (78) sts until the sleeve measures 17 (18) inches in total. Shape the raglan

armhole as follows: Dec 1 st at each edge on every knit row 15 (18) ×. Now dec 1 st at each edge on every row until 1 st remains and the sleeve cap measures 10 (11) inches.

FINISHING

1. With the right sides of back and front facing, sew the side seams.
2. Fold the sleeve with the right side toward the inside. Sew the seam. Turn the sleeve so that the right side is on the outside.
3. With the right sides facing each other, sew the raglan sleeve armhole to the sweater armhole.
4. With #7 16-inch circular needle, starting at the left shoulder, with the right side of the sweater facing you, pick up 8 sts on the left neck edge, knit the 20 sts from the st holder, pick up 8 sts on the right neck edge, knit 32 sts from the back st holder. Place a ring marker and work in k1, p1 rounds for 1½ inches. Bind off loosely in pattern.

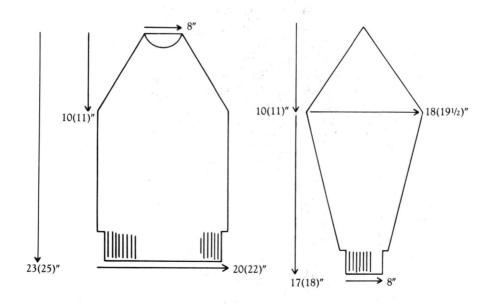

Checkerboard Scarf

This scarf looks well with both Sprinkles (see page 20) and Knit 1 Tuck 1 (see page 46)

SIZE: 10 inches wide by any desired length

MATERIALS:
  Pingouin Jarré 5 (50 g/1.75 ounce) skeins, black/white
  Needles: #9 single-point

GAUGE: 16 sts and 20 rows = 4 inches
  (4 sts = 1 inch; 5 rows = 1 inch)

STITCH PATTERN:
  Row 1: k10, p10, repeat.
  Row 2: k10, p10, repeat.
  Repeat these 2 rows 4× more.
  Row 11: p10, k10, repeat.
  Row 12: p10, k10, repeat.
  Repeat these 2 rows 4× more.
  These 20 rows form the pattern.

SCARF

With #9 needles, cast on 40 sts. Work in pattern stitch until the scarf measures the desired length. Bind off in pattern loosely.

Cut 16-inch pieces for the fringe. With 4 pieces together, folded in half, using a crochet hook, pull the center of the folded threads through the scarf edge. Now bring the ends through the loop tightly. Place the fringes 1" apart. When all the threads have been placed, cut the threads evenly at the bottom.

Magnifico

SIZES: One size

FINISHED MEASUREMENTS: Bust 50 inches; total length 27 inches

MATERIALS:

Knitting Fever/Noro Haruna 13 (50 g/1.75 ounce) skeins, multi navy/red

Needles: #6, #8 single-point

GAUGE: 16 rows and 22 rows = 4 inches (4 sts = 1 inch; 5.5 rows = 1 inch)

STITCH PATTERN:

Stockinette stitch

BACK

With smaller needles (#6), cast on 100 sts. Work k1, p1 rib for 2½ inches. Change to larger needles (#8) and st st and work until the back measures 15 inches in total. Place yarn or coil markers at each edge. Continue in st st until the back measures 27 inches, including the rib. Bind off all sts loosely.

FRONT

Work the front the same as the back until the piece measures 15 inches. Place yarn or coil markers at each edge. Continue to work for ½ inch more. Now divide for the V neck as follows: Work 50 sts, attach a new skein of yarn, and work the last 50 sts. Working both sides at the same time, but with 2 separate skeins of yarn, dec at the front neck edge 1 st on every 3rd row (work 2 rows and then the dec row) 16× until 34 sts remain on each shoulder. Continue to work until the front measures the same as the back. Bind off all sts loosely.

SLEEVES

With smaller needles (#6), cast on 40 sts. Work k1, p1 rib for 3 inches. Change to larger needles (#8) and st st, and inc 12 sts evenly across the first row (52 sts). Working in st st, inc 1 st at each edge on every 3rd row (work 2 rows, then the inc row) 22× (96 sts). Work until the sleeve measures 17–18 inches in total. Bind off all sts loosely.

COLLAR

With larger needles (#8), cast on 10 sts. Work k1, p1 rib. At the beginning of the next row and every 2nd row, cast on 10 sts until there are 50 sts. Make sure that all the cast-on sts have been cast on at the same edge. Work in k1, p1 rib for 30 inches. Bind off all sts loosely in pattern.

FINISHING

1. With the right sides of back and front facing, pin and sew the shoulder seams.
2. Open and lay out flat the back and front with the right side facing up. The yarn markers will still be attached to the sweater.
3. Fold the sleeve in half to find the center of the bound-off edge (the wider side of the length of the sleeve). With the right side facing down,

25

pin the center of the bound-off edge of the sleeve to the shoulder seam of the sweater. The sleeve is now lying across the sweater, covering the neck opening. The bound-off edge of the sleeve will be parallel to the side edge of the sweater, lining up with the markers. Pin the sleeve into the area between the marker on the front and the marker on the back. Pin the body and the sleeve together, being careful not to stretch one side more than the other. Sew the seam.

4. Fold the sweater so that the right side is on the inside. Starting at the underarm, pin the sleeve seams and then the side seams. Sew the seams.

5. Set the collar into the neck opening with the seam on the w s, placing the slanted edge at the center V on the left front and allowing the opposite collar edge to overlap 4 inches beyond the center of the V onto the left-front r s neck edge. Sew the collar. The slanted edge of the collar does not get sewn down.

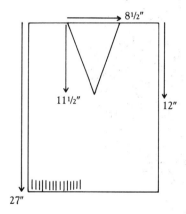

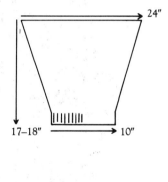

INTERMEDIATE

Play It Again

SIZES: Medium, large; large size is in parentheses

FINISHED MEASUREMENTS: Bust 42 (45) inches; total length 25 inches

MATERIALS

(A) Berger du Nord Lin et Coton 8 (9) (50 g/1.75 ounce) skeins, beige

(B) Lane Borgosesia Rustico 4 (5) (50g/1.75 ounce) skeins, beige/black

(C) Knitting Fever/Noro Katoreya 4 (50 g/1.75 ounce) skeins, cream

Needles: #5, #7, single-point; #5 24-inch circular

GAUGE: 16 sts and 20 rows = 4 inches (4 sts = 1 inch; 5 rows = 1 inch)

STITCH PATTERNS:

#1: Rickrack Rib

Multiples of 3 sts + 1

Row 1: (r s) pl, *with right-hand needle behind the left-hand needle, skip the first stitch and knit into the back of the loop of the second stitch, then knit the skipped stitch through the front loop. Slip both stitches from the needle tog, p1*. Repeat from * to *.

Row 2: (w s) k1, *with yarn in front, skip the first stitch and purl the second stitch, then purl the skipped stitch. Slip both stitches from the needle tog, k1*. Repeat from * to *.

Repeat these 2 rows to form the pattern.

#2: stockinette stitch sequence

Using B, work 10 rows st st (1 row knit, 1 row purl).

Using C, work 4 rows garter st (all knit).

Using A, work 10 rows st st.

Using C, work 4 rows garter st.

Repeat this sequence throughout.

BACK

With smaller needles (#5) and B, cast on 88 (94) sts and work in pattern stitch #1 for 10 rows. Change to A and work 10 rows in pattern #1. Repeat B and A one more time until the Rickrack Rib measures 8 inches. Change to larger needles (#7) and pattern stitch #2, and inc 4 (6) sts evenly spaced across the first knit row (92 [100] sts). Work in color and pattern stitch #2 sequence until the sweater measures 15 inches. Place yarn or coil markers at each edge. Continue to work until the back measures 25 inches in total. Bind off all sts loosely.

FRONT

Work the same as the back until the front measures 19 inches. Now shape the neck as follows: Work 34 (38) sts. Attach a new skein of yarn and

bind off the center 24 sts loosely. Work the last 34 (38) sts. Working each side with a separate skein of yarn, continue the pattern stitch #2 sequence and dec 1 st at each neck edge on every 3rd row (work 2 rows and then the dec row) 8× (26 [30] sts). Continue to work until the front measures the same as the back. Bind off all sts loosely.

FINISHING

1. With the right sides of back and front facing each other, pin and sew the shoulder seams.
2. Armhole bands: Using smaller needles (#5) and B, pick up 79 sts in the space between the two markers on each armhole edge. Work pattern stitch #1, starting with row 2 (w s). Work until the band measures 4 inches. Bind off all the sts loosely in pattern. Fold the bands inward and loosely sew down.
3. Collar: Using #5 24-inch circular needle and B, with the right side facing you, pick up 148 sts around the neck. Work in pattern stitch #1, starting with row 1 (r s). Do not work the collar in rounds; always turn the work after completing 1 row. The collar remains open on one side. Work until the collar measures 8 inches. Using a larger needle, bind off all the sts very loosely in pattern.
4. With the right sides facing inward, pin and sew the side seams.

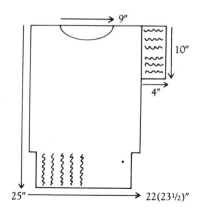

Inca

SIZES: Medium, large; large size is in parentheses

FINISHED MEASUREMENTS: Chest 44 (48) inches. Total length 26 (27) inches

MATERIALS:
  Berger du Nord Shetland 17 (19) (50 g/1.75 ounce) skeins, maize
  Needles: #6, #8 single-point; #6 31-inch circular
  6 buttons

GAUGE: 16 sts and 24 rows = 4 inches (4 sts = 1 inch; 6 rows = 1 inch)

STITCH PATTERN:
  Multiples of 8 sts + 2
  2CL = 2 sts crossed to the left; the italic portion will explain.
  2CR = 2 sts crossed to the right; the italic portion will explain.
  Row 1: k1, k2, p2, *k the 2nd st behind the first st, then k the first st (2CL), p2, k2, p2*. Repeat from * to *, ending with 2CL, p2, k2, k1.
  Row 2: k1, p2, k2, p the 2nd st in front of the first st, then p the first st (2CR), *k2, p2, k2, 2CR*. Repeat from * to *, ending with k2, p2, k1.
  Repeat these 2 rows for the pattern.

BACK

With smaller needles (#6), cast on 106 (122) sts. Work k1, p1 rib for 2½ inches. Change to larger needles (#8) and pattern stitch. Work until the back measures 14 (15) inches in total. Place yarn or coil markers at each edge. Continue in pattern until the back measures 25 (26) inches in total. Shape the shoulders as follows: Bind off 18 (22) sts at the beginning of the next 4 rows. Bind off the remaining 34 sts loosely.

POCKETS

Work the pockets as follows: With #8 needles, cast on 20 sts and work a pocket lining in st st for 3½ inches. Change to the pattern stitch and work 1 inch more. Make two of these pocket linings and set them aside.

RIGHT FRONT

With smaller needles (#6), cast on 58 (66) sts. Work k1, p1 rib for 2½ inches. Change to larger needles (#8) and pattern stitch, and work until the front measures 7 inches in total. Work in the pockets as follows: Work 18 (22) sts in pattern. Work 20 sts in k1, p1 rib. Turn the needles and work across these 20 sts only until this pocket rib measures 1 inch. Bind off all 20 sts loosely in pattern. Reattach the yarn to the sts on the left side of the pocket rib, and in pattern work 20 (24) sts. Turn; work 20 (24) sts. With the WRONG SIDE of the pocket lining facing you, work the 20 sts in pattern, replacing the sts used for the pocket rib. Work the last 18 (22) sts. This is the pocket opening completed. Continue to work until the front measures 14 (15) inches. Place coil or yarn markers at the armhole edge. Work 1 inch more and start shaping the V neck as follows: *Maintain the first 3 sts in pattern and dec after these 3 sts.* At the neck edge, dec 1 st on every 4th row (work 3 rows and then the dec row) 22 (22) ×. Work across the remaining 36 (44) sts until the front measures the same length as the back. Shape the shoulders, binding off loosely 18 (22) sts at the beginning of every second row (at the armhole edge, not the neck edge).

LEFT FRONT

Make the same as the right front, reversing neck shaping and pocket placement.

SLEEVES

With smaller needles (#6), cast on 42 sts. Work k1, p1 rib for 1½ inches. Change to larger needles (#8) and the pattern stitch. Start shaping the sleeves, remembering to work the incs 3 sts away from the edges on each side. Inc 1 st at each edge on every 3rd row (work 2 rows and then the inc row) until 88 sts. Work until the sleeve measures 20 (22) inches in total. Bind off all sts loosely in pattern.

FINISHING

1. Because of the elasticity of this pattern stitch, the pieces must be blocked before finishing the garment. If you are not expert at this technique, ask your local yarn store or dry cleaner to do it.

2. With the right sides of back and front facing, pin and sew the shoulder seams.

3. Open and lay out flat the back and front with the right side facing up. The yarn markers will still be attached to the sweater.

4. Fold the sleeve in half to find the center of the bound-off edge (the wider side of the length of the sleeve). With the right side facing down, pin the center of the bound-off edge of the sleeve to the shoulder seam of the sweater. The sleeve is now lying across the sweater, covering the neck opening. The bound-off edge of the sleeve will be parallel to the side edge of the sweater, lining up with the markers. Pin the sleeve into the area between the marker on the front and the marker on the back. Pin the body and the sleeve together, being careful not to stretch one side more than the other. Sew the seam.

5. Fold the sweater so that the right side is on the inside. Starting at the underarm, pin the sleeve seams and then the side seams. Sew the seams.

6. With the right side facing you, using a #6 31-inch circular needle, pick up 120 sts along the right front edge, 34 sts along the back neck,

and 120 sts along the left front edge. Work k1, p1 rib for 5 rows. Make buttonholes on the left front edge as follows: Work 3 sts *yo, k2 tog, work 12 sts*. Repeat from * to * 5 more times, making 6 buttonholes in total. The last buttonhole should be at the 14-inch length where the neckline is decreased for the first time. On the next row all the yo's will be worked in pattern. Work until the band measures 2 inches. Bind off all sts loosely in pattern.

7. Loosely sew the pocket lining to the body of the sweater, stretching the sweater slightly. Sew the pocket rib.

8. Sew on the buttons.

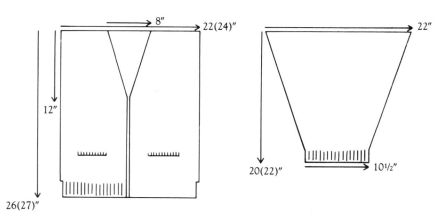

Dimples

SIZES: Small, medium; medium size is in parentheses

FINISHED MEASUREMENTS: Bust 40 (44) inches; total length 24 (25) inches

MATERIALS:
  (A) Berger du Nord Kid mohair 8 (9) (50 g/1.75 ounce) skeins, peach
  (B) Melrose Fresco 1 (50 g/1.75 ounce) skein, blue tweed
  (C) Stacy Charles Rosita 2 (50 g/1.75 ounce) skein, blue
  For sleeves: (A) Kid mohair 4 (5) (50 g/1.75 ounce) skeins, peach
  Needles: #7, #8, #9 single-point
  Stitch holders, markers, buttons

GAUGE: 18 sts and 20 rows = 4 inches (4.5 sts = 1 inch; 5 rows = 1 inch)
  This gauge applies to both stitch patterns.
  When making your swatch, use #9 for the Dimple Stitch.
  When making your swatch, use #8 for the Grid Stitch.

STITCH PATTERNS:
  #1: Grid Stitch
  Rows 1, 2: With A, knit.
  Row 3: With B, k2 *sl 1, k2*. Repeat, ending with k2.
  Row 4: With B, *yf, sl 1, yb, k2*. Repeat, ending with k2.

Rows 5, 6: Repeat rows 3 and 4.
Rows 7, 8: Repeat rows 1 and 2.
Repeat rows 1–8 for the pattern, alternating B and C. A remains constant.

#2: Dimple Stitch
With A:
Row 1: (r s) Knit.
Rows 2, 4: (w s) k1, *sl 3 wyif, p3*. Repeat, ending with sl 3, k1.
Row 3: k1, *sl 3 wyib, k3*. Repeat, ending with sl 3, k1.
Rows 5, 7: Knit.
Row 6: Purl.
Row 8: k1, p1, *insert needle from below under the 3 loose strands of rows 2, 3, and 4, and knit each stitch, bringing the stitch out under the strands, p5*. Repeat, ending with p1, k1.
Row 9: Knit.
Rows 10, 12: k1, *p3, sl 3 wyif*. Repeat, ending p3, k1.
Row 11: k4, *sl 3 wyib, k3*. Repeat, ending k1.
Rows 13, 15: Knit.
Row 14: Purl.
Row 16: k1, p4, *knit the next stitch under the 3 loose strands of rows 10, 11, and 12, p5*. Repeat, ending p4, k1.
Repeat rows 1–16 for the pattern.

BACK

With smaller needles (#7) and A, cast on 90 (96) sts. Work in k1, p1 rib for 1½ inches. On the last rib row, inc 9 sts evenly spaced across the row (99 [105] sts). Change to larger needles (#9) and pattern stitch #2, and work until the piece measures 12 (13) inches. Place yarn or coil markers at each edge. Continue to work until the back measures 24 (25) inches. End the pattern on a knit row. Bind off all sts loosely.

RIGHT FRONT

With smaller needles (#7) and A, cast on 47 (50) sts. Work in k1, p1 rib for 1½ inches. Change to larger needles (#8) and pattern stitch #1. Work 6 grids and then make the pocket as follows: Work 36 (39) sts in pattern. Place the last 20 sts just worked on a st holder, work to the end of the row in pattern (11 sts). Turn and work 11 sts, turn your work so that the needles are in the opposite direction, and cast on 20 sts; turn work, and work the last 16 (19) sts on the row. Work until the front measures 12 (13) inches and place yarn or coil markers at the armhole edge. Now begin to shape the neck. *Remember to maintain your pattern throughout the decreasing.* Dec 1 st at the neck edge on every 7th row (work 6 rows and then the dec row) 11× until 37 (40) sts remain. Work in pattern until the front measures the same as the back. With A, bind off all the sts loosely.

LEFT FRONT

Make the same as the right front, reversing neck shaping and pocket placement.

BUTTON BANDS

With smaller needles (#7), cast on 10 sts. Work in k1, p1 rib for 12 (13) inches. On the left edge, inc 1 st on every 4th row until 20 sts. Work until the band measures 26½ (27½) inches. Bind off all sts loosely in pattern.

For the left button band with buttonholes:

With smaller needles (#7), cast on 10 sts. Work 3 rows k1, p1 rib.

Next row: Work 4 sts, bind off 2 sts, work 4 sts.

Next row: Work 4 sts, turn work and cast on 2 sts, turn work, work 4 sts. Work for 2 inches and then make another buttonhole. Repeat until 5 (6) buttonholes are made and band measures 12 (13) inches. On the right edge, inc 1 st on every 4th row until 20 sts. Work until the band measures 26½ (27½) inches. Bind off all sts loosely in pattern.

ARMHOLE BANDS

Sew the shoulder seams. With larger needles (#8), pick up 119 sts in between the markers at the armhole edge. Work pattern stitch #2, starting with row 1 on the w s. Work for 4 inches. Bind off all sts loosely.

As an alternative, you can make sleeves instead of armhole bands.

SLEEVES

With smaller needles (#7) and A, cast on 40 sts. Work k1, p1 rib for 1½ inches. Change to larger needles (#9) and pattern stitch #2. Inc 1 st at the beginning of the first pattern row. At each edge, inc 1 st on every 4th row (work 3 rows and then the inc row) until 83 sts. Continue in pattern until the sleeve measures 19 (20) inches or the desired length. Bind off all sts loosely.

FINISHING

1. With the right sides of back and front facing, pin and sew the shoulder seams.
2. Open and lay out flat the back and front with the right side facing up. The yarn markers will still be attached to the sweater.
3. Fold the sleeve in half to find the center of the bound-off edge (the wider side of the length of the sleeve). With the right side facing down, pin the center of the bound-off edge of the sleeve to the shoulder seam of the sweater. The sleeve is now lying across the sweater, covering the neck opening. The bound-off edge of the sleeve will be parallel to the side edge of the sweater, lining up with the markers. Pin the sleeve into the area between the marker on the front and the marker on the back. Pin the body and the sleeve together, being careful not to stretch one side more than the other. Sew the seam.

4. Fold the sweater so that the right side is on the inside. Starting at the underarm, pin the sleeve seams and then the side seams. Sew the seams.
5. Place the pocket sts from the st holder onto smaller needles (#7) and work k1, p1 rib for 1 inch. Separately work 2 pocket linings in st st; cast on 20 sts and work for 3 inches. Bind off. Sew this lining to the front pocket section, making sure that the knit side faces the w s of the sweater.
6. Fold armhole bands toward the inside and loosely sew down.
7. Sew the button bands together and center the seam at the back of the neck. Pin the bands to the front bottom edges and then ease the rest of the bands to fit the front neck edges. Pin and sew. Remember to place the buttonholes on the right side. The shaped edge of the button bands should be attached to the body of the sweater.
8. Sew the buttons on.

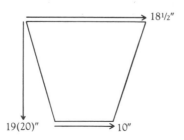

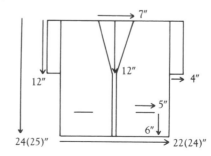

Fluffy

SIZES: One size

FINISHED MEASUREMENTS: Bust 46
  inches; total length 20 inches

MATERIALS:
  (A) Chanteleine Blondine 8 (50 g/1.75
    ounce) skeins, pink
  (B) Knitting Fever/Noro Hakucho 2 (20 g)
    boxes, 1 white, 1 taupe
  Needles: #10½ single-point

GAUGE: 8 sts and 12 rows = 4 inches
        (2 sts = 1 inch; 3 rows = 1 inch)

STITCH PATTERN:
  Stockinette stitch

HINTS:

Follow the graph when working with B.

Do not cut the A thread when working with B;
just carry it behind the work.

This sweater is made in 2 pieces.

LEFT SIDE:

With #10½ needles, cast on 46 sts. Work in k1,
p1 rib for 6 rows. Change to st st and work until
the piece measures 12 inches. At the beginning
of the next purl row, cast on 40 sts (to make 86
sts) for the sleeve. Maintain the first 6 sts in k1,
p1 rib and all the other sts in st st. Work until the
sleeve measures 16 inches in length. Bind off 40

sts at the beginning of the next purl row. Continue to work another 11 inches in st st for the
back and then work k1, p1 rib for 6 rows. Bind
off all sts loosely in pattern.

RIGHT SIDE

Work this piece the same as the left side, reversing all the shaping; cast on 40 sts on a knit row.

FINISHING

1. Sew the front seams for 11 inches. Do the
  same on the back.
2. Sew the sleeve seams and the side seams.
3. Fold the cuff 2 or 3 times.

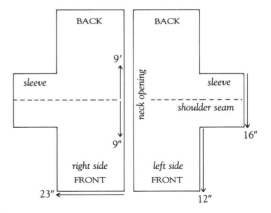

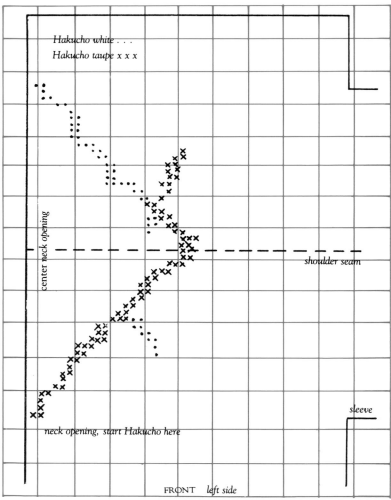

Each square represents 5 stitches and 5 rows.

40

Eleganza

SIZES: One size

FINISHED MEASUREMENTS: Bust 48 inches; total length 20 inches

MATERIALS:
Pingouin Jarré 10 (50 g/1.75 ounce) skeins, beige

Needles: #9 single-point

GAUGE: 13 sts and 18 rows = 4 inches (3.25 sts = 1 inch; 4.5 rows = 1 inch)

STITCH PATTERN:
Row 1: *k4, p2*. Repeat from * to *, ending with k4.

Row 2: *p4, k2*. Repeat from * to *, ending with p4.

Repeat these 2 rows for the pattern.

BACK

With #9 needles, cast on 106 sts. Work in pattern stitch until the back measures 8 inches. Place yarn or coil markers at each edge. Continue to work in pattern until the back measures 20 inches. Bind off all sts loosely in pattern.

RIGHT FRONT

With #9 needles, cast on 52 sts. Work in pattern stitch until piece measures 8 inches. Place yarn or coil markers at the armhole edge. Work for 1½

inches more. At the neck edge dec 1 st on every 4th row 10× (42 sts), *maintaining the first 6 stitches in pattern to keep the edge smooth.* Work until the front measures 20 inches, the same length as the back. Bind off all sts loosely.

LEFT FRONT

Make the same as the right front, reversing neck shaping.

SLEEVE CUFF

With #9 needles, cast on 24 sts. Work in pattern stitch until the cuff measures 8 inches. Bind off all sts loosely.

SLEEVE

With #9 needles, cast on 46 sts. Work in pattern stitch, and inc 1 st at each edge on every 4th row (work 3 rows and then the inc row) 12× (70 sts). Work until the sleeve measures 14 inches. Bind off all sts loosely.

FINISHING

1. With the right sides of back and front facing, pin and sew the shoulder seams.

2. Open and lay out flat the back and front with the right side facing up. The yarn markers will still be attached to the sweater.

3. Fold the sleeve in half to find the center of the bound-off edge (the wider side of the length of the sleeve). With the right side facing down, pin the center of the bound-off edge of the sleeve to the shoulder seam of the sweater. The sleeve is now lying across the sweater, covering the neck opening. The bound-off edge of the sleeve will be parallel to the side edge of the sweater, lining up with the markers. Pin the sleeve into the area between the marker on the front and the marker on the back. Pin the body and the sleeve together, being careful not to stretch one side more than the other. Sew the seam.

4. Fold the sweater so that the right side is on the inside. Starting at the underarm, pin the sleeve seams and then the side seams. Sew the seams.

5. On the right front, with the w s facing, crochet 5 button loops ½ inch from the edge as follows: single crochet, chain 5, single crochet. Space the loops 2½ inches apart.

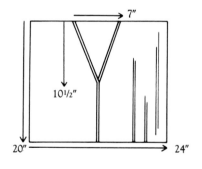

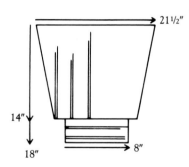

ADVANCED

Knit 1 Tuck 1

SIZES: One size
FINISHED MEASUREMENTS: Bust 50 inches; total length 25 inches
MATERIALS
   Pingouin Brigantin 24 (50 g/1.75 ounce) skeins, black/white
   Needles: #10½ single-point
GAUGE: 9 sts and 14 rows = 4 inches (2.25 sts = 1 inch; 3.5 rows = 1 inch)
STITCH PATTERN:
   Stockinette stitch

BACK

With #10½ needles, cast on 74 sts. Work 3 rows garter st. Change to st st and work until piece measures 3 inches in total. Inc 1 st at each edge on every 4th row (work 3 rows and then the inc row) 4× (to make 82 sts). *At the same time* when the piece measures 10 inches make the tuck as follows on the w s (purl row): p38, pick up the next st 3½ inches below the needle, place the k st on the left needle, and purl the st together with the next st. Repeat this step 5× more, purl the last 38 sts. Continue to work in st st until the back measures 12 inches. Work the short rows as follows:

   Row 1: k50, turn.
   Row 2: p18, turn.

   Row 3: k19, turn.
   Row 4: p20, turn.
   Row 5: k21, turn.
   Row 6: p22, turn.

Continue in this short-row manner until p28, turn, knit to the end of the row. Work across all sts until the piece measures 13 inches. On the first dec row, use about 12 inches of yarn in another color, knitting it along in the center of the row for about 10 sts. This is used to assist in the measuring of the armhole and is removed when the sweater is finished. Bind off 3 sts at the beginning of the next 2 rows (76 sts). At each edge, on the next 2 knit rows, dec 1 st 2× (72 sts). Work until the armhole measures 12 inches. Bind off all sts loosely.

RIGHT FRONT

With #10½ needles, cast on 7 sts. Knit 2 rows, turn, cast on 7 sts. Knit 1 row, turn, k7, p7, turn, cast on 7 sts, k21, turn, p14, k7, turn, cast on 7 sts, k28 sts, turn, p21, k7.

   Maintaining the first 2 sts as knit sts at the center front edge throughout the sweater, work 2 rows st st.

   NOTE 1. For buttonholes, work as follows: k2, yo, k2 tog, k to end. Buttonholes are spaced 3 inches apart.

NOTE 2. The center front increases should be made after the first 2 knit sts.

Working the first buttonhole immediately, start the shaping as follows: Inc 1 st at each edge of the next knit row and every 4th knit row (work 7 rows and then the inc row) 4× (36 sts). Continue to inc at the center front edge only on every 6th row (work 5 rows and then the inc row)

9×. When, measuring the longest side, the front measures 13 inches, bind off 3 sts at the armhole edge. On the next 2 knit rows, dec at the armhole edge 1 st 2×. Remember to continue increasing at the center front edge. Work until the armhole measures 9 inches. Bind off loosely 14 sts at the neck edge. Then dec 1 st on every row at the neck edge 3×. Continue to work until the armhole measures 12 inches. Bind off all sts loosely.

LEFT FRONT

With #10½ needles, cast on 7 sts. Knit 1 row, turn. Knit 1 row, turn, cast on 7 sts, k7, p14, turn, knit 1 row, turn, cast on 7 sts, k7, p21, turn, knit 1 row, purl 1 row, maintaining the 2 center front edge sts as knit sts. Work the left front as the right front, reversing all the shapings. The left front has no buttonholes.

SLEEVES

With #10½ needles, cast on 34 sts. Work garter stitch for 5 rows. Change to st st and inc 1 st at each edge on every 5th row 12× (58 sts). Continue to work until the sleeve measures 18 inches. At the beginning of the next 2 rows, bind off 4 sts (50 sts). Work 6 rows st st. Dec 1 st at each edge on every knit row until 14 sts remain and the sleeve cap measures 10 inches. Bind off all sts loosely.

FINISHING

1. With the right sides of back and front facing, pin and sew the shoulder seams.
2. Pin and sew the side seams.
3. Following the diagram, place the braid into the sleeves. Sew the sleeve seams and, with the wrong side facing you, set the sleeves into the armholes, matching up the underarm seams and centering the top of the sleeve to match the shoulder seam.
4. Sew on the buttons.

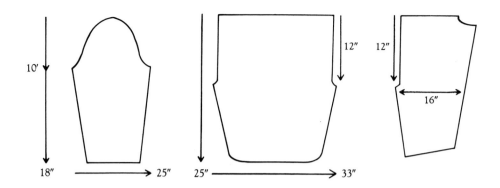

10' 18" ➝ 25"

12"

25" ➝ 33"

12"

16"

H
G   1"
F
E   2"
   1"
D   2"
C
B   1"
   2"
A   6"

A and H knot only. B,C,D,E,F,
and G knot and hole.

Bellhop Jacket

SIZES: Small, medium; medium size is in parentheses

FINISHED MEASUREMENTS: Bust 40 (44) inches; total length 20 (21) inches

This jacket can be made in many different yarns. Here are 2 variations, a summer and a winter version.

MATERIALS: Summer cotton
- (A) Melrose Delavo 5 (6) (50 g/1.75 ounce) skeins, burnt orange
- (B) Melrose Spigetta 3 (4) (100 g/3.5 ounce) skeins, pink
- (C) Pingouin Viscosa 2 (50 g/1.75 ounce) skeins, gray

MATERIALS: Winter angora
- (A) Laines Anny Blatt Angora 16 (10 g/.7 ounce) skeins, black
- (B) Laines Anny Blatt Angora 11 (10 g/.7 ounce) skeins, wine
- (C) Pingouin Viscosa 2 (50 g/1.75 ounce) skeins, saffron

Needles: #8 single-point
Crochet hook: size F

GAUGE: 16 sts and 20 rows = 4 inches (4 sts = 1 inch; 5 rows = 1 inch)

STITCH PATTERN:
Stockinette stitch

NOTE: When changing colors, twist yarns on the wrong side to prevent holes.

BACK

With #8 needles and A, cast on 4 (8) sts, with B cast on 46 sts, and with A cast on 30 (34) sts (80 [88] sts). Following the graph, work in st st, in the designated colors. When the back measures 11 (12) inches, place yarn or coil markers at each edge. Work until the piece measures 20 (21) inches in total length. Bind off all sts loosely, using A and B in the correct places.

RIGHT FRONT

With #8 needles and A, cast on 17 (21) sts, and with B, cast on 23 sts (40 [44] sts). Following the graph, work until the front measures 11 (12) inches. Place yarn or coil markers at the armhole edge. When the front measures 12 inches, start shaping the neck edge as follows: Inc 1 st on every 3rd row (work 2 rows and then the inc row) 10×, then inc 1 st on every 2nd row 5× (55 [59] sts). Work until the piece measures 20 (21) inches. Bind off all sts loosely.

LEFT FRONT

With #8 needles and A, cast on 23 (27) sts, and with B, cast on 17 sts (40 [44] sts). Work as for right front, reversing the shaping for the neck edge, but follow the chart for the left front.

SLEEVES

Make one sleeve using A and one sleeve using B.

With #8 needles, cast on 38 sts. Working in st st, inc 1 st at each edge on every 4th row (work 3 rows and then the inc row) 20× (78 sts). Work until the sleeve measures 19 (20) inches. Bind off all sts loosely.

FINISHING

1. With the right sides of back and front facing, pin and sew the shoulder seams.
2. Open and lay out flat the back and front with the right side facing up. The yarn markers will still be attached to the sweater.

3. Fold the sleeve in half to find the center of the bound-off edge (the wider side of the length of the sleeve). With the right side facing down, pin the center of the bound-off edge of the sleeve to the shoulder seam of the sweater. The sleeve is now lying across the sweater, covering the neck opening. The bound-off edge of the sleeve will be parallel to the side edge of the sweater, lining up with the markers. Pin the sleeve into the area between the marker on the front and the marker on the back. Pin the body and the sleeve together, being careful not to stretch one side more than the other. Sew the seam.

4. Fold the sweater so that the right side is on the inside. Starting at the underarm, pin the sleeve seams and then the side seams. Sew the seams.

5. Crochet trimming: With F hook and C, with the right side facing you, work 3 single crochet into each stitch. Work this all the way around the outer edge of the jacket, the wrist opening, and on the body of the jacket where the 2 colors meet.

6. Button loops are crocheted at the areas specified on the chart. Method: chain 5, skip 2 sts, and single crochet as step 5.

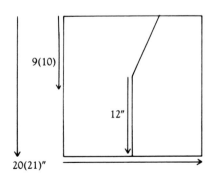

9(10)

12"

20(21)"

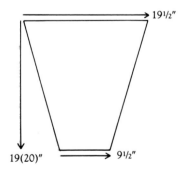

19½"

19(20)"

9½"

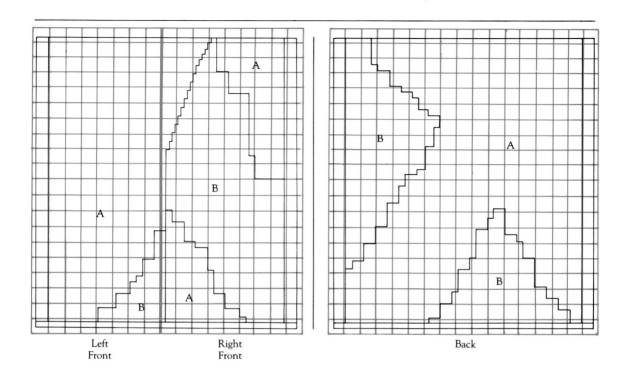

Left Front		Right Front		Back

Each square represents 5 stitches and 5 rows.

Jimmy!

SIZES: Medium, large; large size is in parentheses

FINISHED MEASUREMENTS: Chest 42 (46) inches; total length 25 (26) inches

MATERIALS:

Knitting Fever/Noro Tachibana 14 (16) (50 g/1.75 ounce) skeins, dark gray

Needles: #9, #10½ single-point, #9 16-inch circular

Stitch holder

GAUGE: 12 sts and 16 rows = 4 inches (3 sts = 1 inch; 4 rows = 1 inch)

STITCH PATTERN:

Row 1: *p9, k3*. Repeat, ending with p3 (p9).

Row 2: Work the sts as they face you; knit the knits and purl the purls.

Rows 3, 4: Repeat rows 1 and 2.

Row 5: k3 *k3, p9*. Repeat, ending with p9 (p9, k6).

Row 6: Knit the knits and purl the purls.

Rows 7, 8: Repeat rows 5 and 6.

Repeat rows 1–8 for the pattern.

BACK

With smaller needles (#9), cast on 60 (66) sts. Work k1, p1 rib for 3 inches. Change to larger needles (#10½) and pattern stitch, and inc 3 sts evenly across the row (63 [69] sts). Work in pattern stitch until the back measures 15 (17) inches. Place yarn or coil markers at each edge. Continue to work until the back measures 24 (25) inches in total. Now shape the shoulders as follows: At the beginning of the next 4 rows, bind off 8 (9) sts. Place the remaining 28 (30) sts on a st holder.

FRONT

Work the front the same as the back until the piece measures 17 (18) inches in total. Now divide for the V neck as follows: Work 31 (34) sts in pattern; place center st on a st holder. Attach a new skein of yarn and work the last 31 (34) sts in pattern. Working both sides at the same time, but with separate skeins of yarn, at the neck edge decrease 1 st on every 2nd row 14 (15) × until 17 (19) sts remain on each shoulder and the front, in total, measures the same as the back. Now shape the shoulders the same as the back.

Sew the shoulders together, straightening the slanted bound-off edges.

SLEEVES

With smaller needles (#9), cast on 28 (30) sts. Work k1, p1 rib for 3 inches. Change to larger needles (#10½) and reverse stockinette stitch (the purl row is the right-side row), and inc 6 sts

evenly across the row. Continue in rev st st, and inc 1 st at each edge on every 6th row (work 5 rows and then the inc row) 13 (12) × (60 sts). Work until the sleeve measures 21 (22) inches. Bind off all sts loosely.

FINISHING

1. With the right sides of back and front facing, pin and sew the shoulder seams.
2. Open and lay out flat the back and front with the right side facing up. The yarn markers will still be attached to the sweater.
3. Fold the sleeve in half to find the center of the bound-off edge (the wider side of the length of the sleeve). With the right side facing down, pin the center of the bound-off edge of the sleeve to the shoulder seam of the sweater. The sleeve is now lying across the sweater, covering the neck opening. The bound-off edge of the sleeve will be parallel to the side edge of the sweater, lining up with the markers. Pin the sleeve into the area between the

marker on the front and the marker on the back. Pin the body and the sleeve together, being careful not to stretch one side more than the other. Sew the seam.

4. Fold the sweater so that the right side is on the inside. Starting at the underarm, pin the sleeve seams and then the side seams. Sew the seams.
5. With the right side facing you, with #9 16-inch circular needle, starting at the left shoulder seam, pick up 28 sts on the left front edge, place a ring marker, k1, place a ring marker, pick up 28 sts on the right front edge, pick up 28 (30) sts across the back edge. Arrange the sts so that the center stitch is a knit stitch. This stitch will remain a knit stitch throughout the neck border. Work rounds in k1, p1 rib, and dec 1 st before the center stitch and dec 1 st after the center stitch. Remember to maintain the pattern after the dec. Dec on every round. When the border measures 1 inch, bind off all sts loosely in pattern, attaching the first and last stitch bound off for a smooth edge.

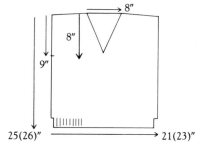

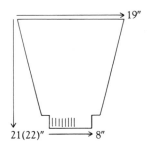

Désirée

SIZES: Small, medium; medium size is in
parentheses
FINISHED MEASUREMENTS: Bust 40
(44) inches; total length 22 (23) inches

MATERIALS:
(A) China Silk Imari 3 (4) (100 g/3.5
ounce) skeins, black
(B) Anny Blatt Angor'anny 10 (12) (20

g/.7 ounce) skeins, black
Needles: #3, #5 single-point
GAUGE: 22 sts and 24 rows = 4 inches
(5.5 sts = 1 inch; 6 rows = 1 inch)

STITCH PATTERNS:

#1

With A, work 2 rows k1, p1 rib.
With B, work 2 rows k1, p1 rib.
Repeat 4 rows for the pattern.

#2

With A, work 4 rows st st.
With B, work 4 rows st st.
Repeat 8 rows for the pattern.

#3: Lace Collar

Using smaller needles (#3) and A, cast on 6 sts.
Row 1: k1, yo 2×, k2 tog., yo 2×, k2 tog, k1.
Row 2: k3, p1, k2, p1, k1.
Row 3: k3, yo 2×, k2 tog, yo 2×, k2 tog, k1.
Row 4: k3, p1, k2, p1, k3.
Row 5: k5, yo 2×, k2 tog, yo 2×, k2 tog, k1.
Row 6: k3, p1, k2, p1, k5.
Row 7: k7, yo 2×, k2 tog, yo 2×, k2 tog, k1.
Row 8: k3, p1, k2, p1, k7.
Row 9: k9, yo 2×, k2 tog, yo 2×, k2 tog, k1.
Row 10: k3, p1, k12.
Rows 11, 12, 13: Knit 16 sts.
Row 14: Bind off 10 sts, k6.
Repeat rows 1–14 until 21 leaves have been made and the collar measures 36 inches. Bind off all sts loosely.

BACK

With smaller needles (#3) and A, cast on 94 (104) sts. Work in pattern #1 until rib measures 3 inches. Change to larger needles (#5) and pattern #2, and inc 18 sts evenly spaced across the first knit row (112 [122] sts). Work until the piece measures 12 inches, and place yarn or coil markers at each edge. Continue until the back measures 22 (23) inches in total. Bind off all sts loosely in pattern.

FRONT

Work as for the back until the piece measures 8½ (9½) inches. Divide for the V neck as follows: Work 47 (52) sts, attach a new skein of yarn, and bind off the center 18 sts. Work the last 47 (52) sts with the second skein of yarn. Working each side separately, at the neck edge, dec 1 st every 5th row (work 4 rows and then the dec row) 17×, until (30 [35] sts) remain for each shoulder. Remember to place markers at each edge when the front measures 12 (13) inches. Work until the front measures the same as the back. Bind off all sts loosely.

SLEEVES

With smaller needles (#3) and A, cast on 44 (54) sts. In pattern stitch #1, work 3 inches. Change to larger needles (#5) and pattern stitch #2, increasing 30 sts evenly across the first knit row (74 [84] sts). Continue to work in pattern #2, increasing 1 st at each edge on every 5th row 13 × (100 [110] sts). Work until the sleeve measures 19 (20) inches. Bind off all sts loosely.

FINISHING

1. With the right sides of back and front facing, pin and sew the shoulder seams.
2. Open and lay out flat the back and front with the right side facing up. The yarn markers will still be attached to the sweater.
3. Fold the sleeve in half to find the center of the bound-off edge (the wider side of the length of the sleeve). With the right side facing down, pin the center of the bound-off edge of the sleeve to the shoulder seam of the sweater.

The sleeve is now lying across the sweater, covering the neck opening. The bound-off edge of the sleeve will be parallel to the side edge of the sweater, lining up with the markers. Pin the sleeve into the area between the marker on the front and the marker on the back. Pin the body and the sleeve together, being careful not to stretch one side more than the other. Sew the seam.

4. Fold the sweater so that the right side is on the inside. Starting at the underarm, pin the sleeve seams and then the side seams. Sew the seams.
5. Sew the lace collar to the neck, setting the flat edge into the center edge of the V neck, allowing the lace leaves to overlap at the front. Overlap and sew the first 3 leaves.

IMPORTANT NOTE

DO NOT BLOCK ANGORA. DO NOT STORE IN A PLASTIC BAG.

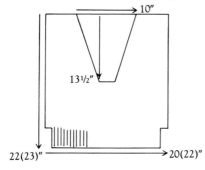

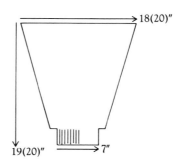

NOTE:

All yarns used in this book can be ordered from:

Gwen Byrne
529 Amsterdam Avenue
New York, N.Y. 10024

All sweaters are also available custom-made. Request a price list, enclosing a stamped, self-addressed envelope.